CREATURES
OF THE NIGHT

LUNA MOTHS

QUINN M. ARNOLD

CREATIVE EDUCATION • CREATIVE PAPERBACKS

CONTENTS

THE DARK OF NIGHT BLANKETS A NORTH AMERICAN FOREST. IT IS PAST MIDNIGHT. TWO LUNA MOTHS MEET AMONG THE **DECIDUOUS** TREES

THE MALE HAS FLOWN SEVERAL MILES IN SEARCH OF THIS FEMALE. HE FOLLOWED THE SCENT SHE RELEASED.

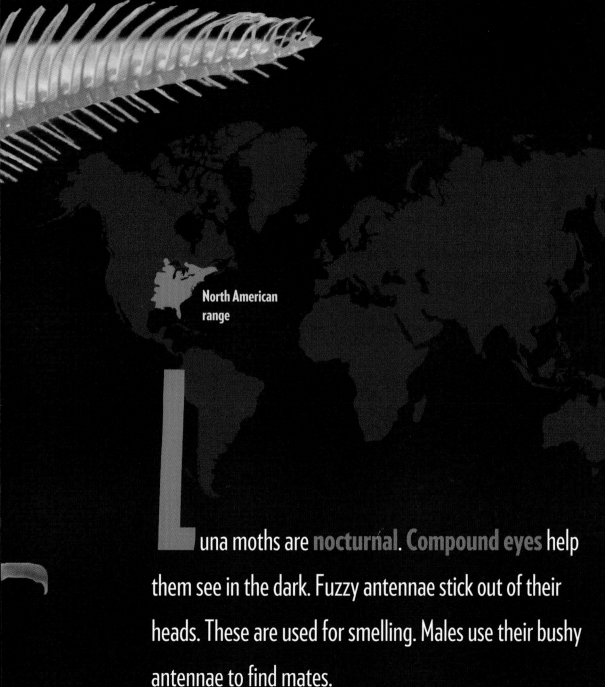

North American range

Luna moths are nocturnal. Compound eyes help them see in the dark. Fuzzy antennae stick out of their heads. These are used for smelling. Males use their bushy antennae to find mates.

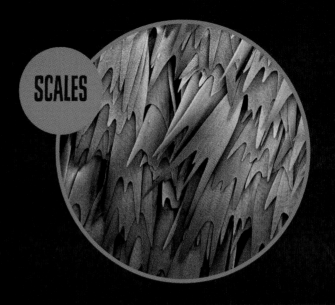

SCALES

Luna moths are insects. They have six pinkish legs and two pairs of wings. The moths' wide wings are green. They are covered with tiny, soft scales. Each wing has a dark eyespot.

A long tail hangs from each hind wing. These tails flutter during flight. They sound like wingbeats. This confuses bats that hunt luna moths.

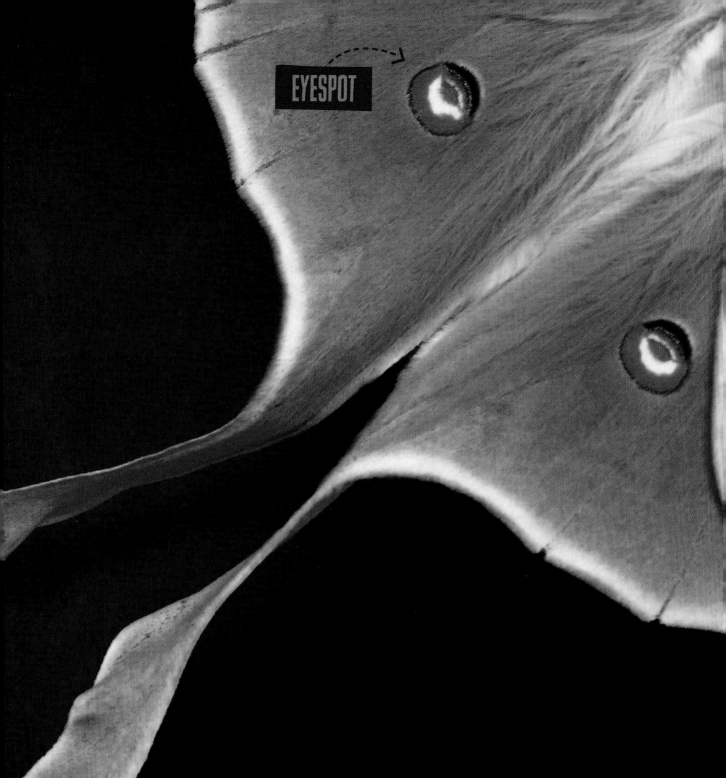

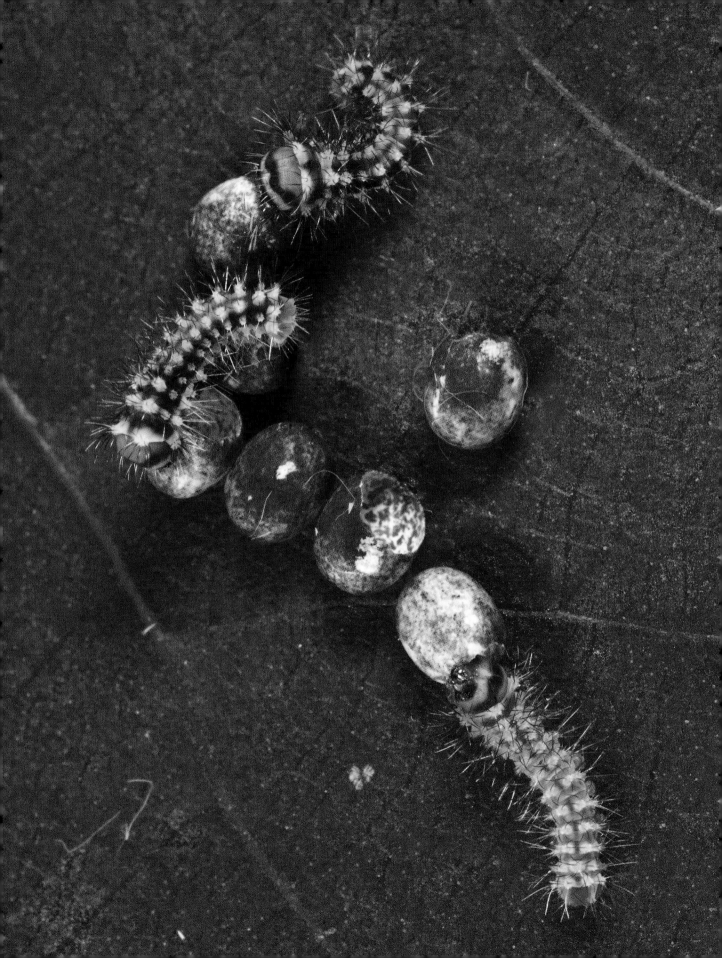

Adult luna moths do not eat. They do not even have mouthparts! As larvae, these creatures take the form of caterpillars. The small, green caterpillars hatch from eggs. They eat a lot.

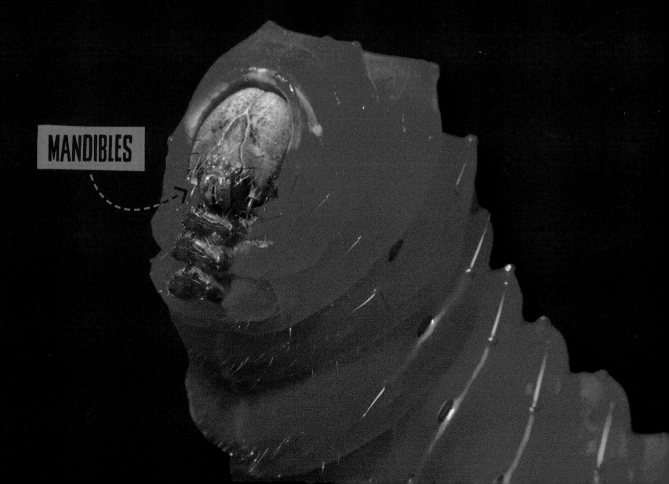

MANDIBLES

Luna moth caterpillars munch on tree leaves. They grow and **molt**. The time between each molt is called an instar. Luna moth caterpillars go through five instars.

1ST INSTAR 6-8 MM

2ND INSTAR 9-10 MM

3RD INSTAR 13-15 MM

4TH INSTAR 23 MM

5TH INSTAR 65 MM

A luna moth caterpillar eats and grows
for about a month. Then, using silk and
bits of leaf, it spins a cocoon. There the
caterpillar will become a moth.

Luna moths break out of cocoons in the morning. Their wings expand and dry during the day. The moths are able to fly by nightfall. Luna moths live for 7 to 10 days. Their only goal is to find mates.

LIFE OF A LUNA MOTH

HATCHES
caterpillar breaks out of egg

MOLTS
eats leaves; undergoes 5 instars

PUPATES
spins a cocoon; becomes an adult moth

HATCHES
breaks out of cocoon as an adult

ADULT
about 4.5 in (11.4 cm) long; reproduces

At dawn, the luna moths part ways. Each finds a resting spot hidden between green leaves. This evening, the female will begin to lay eggs. The male will search for a new mate.

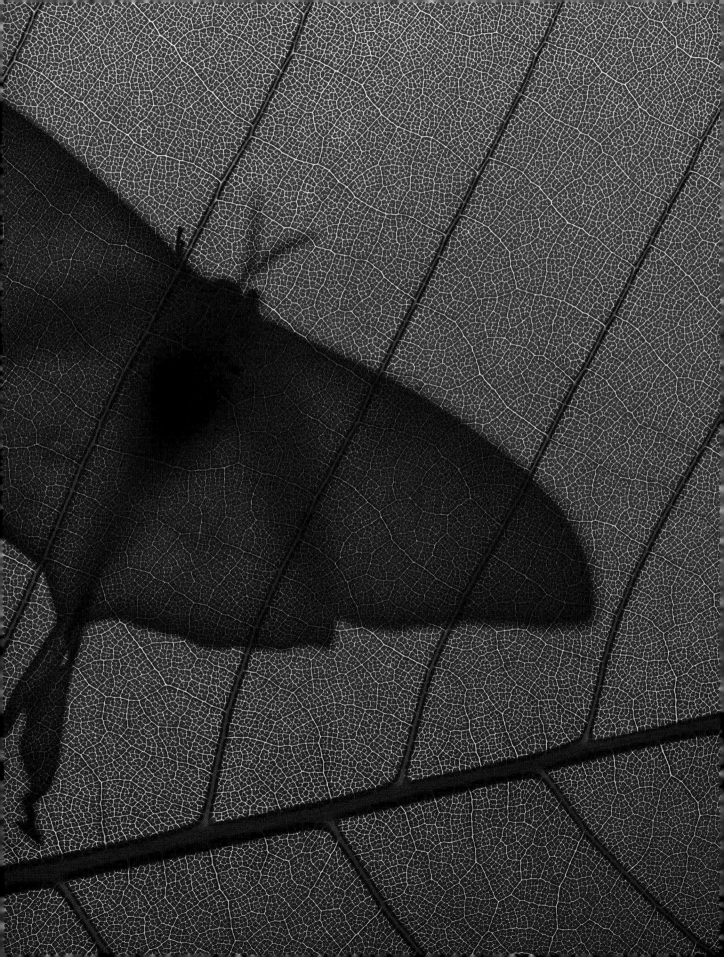

TAILS

hanging from each hind
wing, tails can double a
luna moth's body length;
tails are not necessary for
flight or survival

BODY ›

large bodies are covered in fuzzy
white hair; females give off a scent
from the rear end of the body—males
follow this scent to locate mates

WINGS
the edges of the green
wings may be rimmed dark
purple or brown, and each
features an eyespot

ANTENNAE
used for smelling; males
have bushier antennae than
females, which they use
to locate females

GLOSSARY

COCOON
a protective case spun from silk produced by a young insect

DECIDUOUS
trees that shed leaves yearly

MOLT
to shed old skin to make room for new growth

COMPOUND EYES
eyes made up of many small visual units

LARVAE
the newly hatched, often wormlike form of many insects

NOCTURNAL
active at night

READ MORE

Merwin, E. *Luna Moth*. New York: Bearport, 2018.

Murawski, Darlyne, and Nancy Honovich. *Ultimate Bugopedia: The Most Complete Bug Reference Ever*. Washington, D.C.: National Geographic, 2013.

Perish, Patrick. *Moths*. Minneapolis: Bellwether Media, 2018.

WEBSITES

DK Find Out!: Butterflies and Moths
https://www.dkfindout.com/us/animals-and-nature/insects/butterflies-and-moths/

National Geographic Kids: Luna Moth
https://kids.nationalgeographic.com/animals/luna-moth/

YouTube: Butterfly or Moth?
https://www.youtube.com/watch?v=iblveeTDkXQ

Note: Every effort has been made to ensure that the websites listed above are suitable for children, that they have educational value, and that they contain no inappropriate material. However, because of the nature of the Internet, it is impossible to guarantee that these sites will remain active indefinitely or that their contents will not be altered.

INDEX

PUBLISHED BY CREATIVE EDUCATION
AND CREATIVE PAPERBACKS

P.O. Box 227, Mankato, Minnesota 56002
Creative Education and Creative Paperbacks
are imprints of The Creative Company
www.thecreativecompany.us

LIBRARY OF CONGRESS
CATALOGING-IN-PUBLICATION DATA

Names: Arnold, Quinn M., author.
Title: Luna moths / Quinn M. Arnold.
Series: Creatures of the night.
Includes index.
Summary: Peer into the nocturnal North American forests with this high-interest introduction to the green-winged insects known as luna moths.

Identifiers:
LCCN: 2018059119
ISBN 978-1-64026-119-8 (hardcover)
ISBN 978-1-62832-682-6 (pbk)
ISBN 978-1-64000-237-1 (eBook)

Subjects: LCSH: Luna moth—Juvenile literature.
Nocturnal animals—Juvenile literature.
Classification: LCC QL561.S2 A76 2019 / DDC 591.5/18—dc23

CCSS: RI.1.1-6; RI.2.1-7; RF.1.1-4; RF.2.1-4

DESIGN AND PRODUCTION

by Joe Kahnke; art direction by Rita Marshall
Printed in the United States of America

PHOTOGRAPHS by Alamy (Paul Bolotov, Katherine Gaines, Grant Heilman Photography, Jeff Lepore, Ilukee, Papilio, Pixels of Nature), Getty Images (Ted Kinsman/Science Source, John Mitchell/Science Source), iStockphoto (AVTG, tshortell), Minden Pictures (Matthias Breiter), National Geographic Image Collection (DOMINIQUE BRAUD/ANIMALS ANIMALS/EARTH SCENES, Al Petteway & Amy White), Science Source (Jeff Lepore), Shutterstock (Breck P. Kent, Stephen Marques)

Images on pages 12 and 13 courtesy of Donald W. Hall,
University of Florida Featured Creatures.

HC 9 8 7 6 5 4 3 2
PBK 9 8 7 6 5 4 3 2 1